Beginning Biographies

Amelia Earhart
Female Aviator

Anne Golightly

PowerKiDS press™

NEW YORK

Published in 2013 by The Rosen Publishing Group, Inc.
29 East 21st Street, New York, NY 10010

Book Design: Michael Harmon

Photo Credits: Cover Pictures Inc./Contributor/Time & Life Pictures/Getty Images; p. 4 http://commons.wikimedia.org/wiki/File:Amelia_earhart.jpeg;
p. 5 SCIENCE SOURCE/Photo Researchers/Getty Images; p. 6 Thinkstock Images/Thinkstock.com; p. 7 Hulton Archive/Stringer/Hulton Archive/Getty Images;
p. 8 iStockphoto/Thinkstock.com; pp. 9, 21 Dorling Kindersley RF/Thinkstock.com; p. 10 New York Times Co./Contributor/Archive Photos/Getty Images;
pp. 11, 13 New York Daily News Archive/Contributor/New York Daily News via Getty Images; p. 14 Fox Studios/Stringer/Hutlon Archive/Getty Images;
p. 15 http://www.whitehousehistory.org/whha_pictures/presidentshouse_hoover-07.html; p. 16 Topical Press Agency/Stringer/Hulton Archive/Getty
Images; p. 17 http://en.wikipedia.org/wiki/File:Earheart,_1928.jpg; p. 18 Creatas/Thinkstock.com; p. 19 http://en.wikipedia.org/wiki/File:AE_and
_Vega.jpg; p. 20 http://en.wikipedia.org/wiki/File:Pacific_Ocean_satellite_image_location_map.jpg.

Library of Congress Cataloging-in-Publication Data

Golightly, Anne.
 Amelia Earhart : female aviator / Anne Golightly.
     p. cm. — (Beginning biographies)
 Includes index.
 ISBN: 978-1-4488-8854-2
 6-pack ISBN: 978-1-4488-8855-9
 ISBN: 978-1-4488-8601-2 (library binding)
 1. Earhart, Amelia, 1897-1937—Juvenile literature. 2. Women air pilots—United States—Biography—Juvenile literature.
 3. Air pilots—United States—Biography—Juvenile literature. I. Title.
 TL540.E3G64 2013
 629.13092—dc23
 [B]
                                        2012012030

Manufactured in the United States of America

CPSIA Compliance Information: Batch #WS12RC: For further information contact Rosen Publishing, New York, New York at 1-800-237-9932.

Word Count: 453

Contents

Female Aviator

Amelia Earhart was a well-known American. Do you know why Amelia was important?

Amelia was an **aviator**. An aviator is someone who flies an airplane. In Amelia's day, men usually did this job. Amelia was one of the first women to fly planes.

Airplanes were new when Amelia was alive.

Very few people had been inside a plane.

Everyone wanted to know what flying was like.

Amelia saw her first plane when she was 10 years old. She didn't think it was that special. Have you ever seen a plane up close?

In 1920, Amelia took her first plane ride. She loved it so much that she decided to buy her own plane! It was small and yellow.

Amelia started taking flying classes. She became really good at flying. People started to notice her. This made Amelia want to fly even more.

Setting Records

Amelia wanted to fly so she could set records. Setting a record means that you do something first or you do it best.

Amelia set many records. She was the first woman aviator to do a lot of important things. Her records made her very **popular** in America.

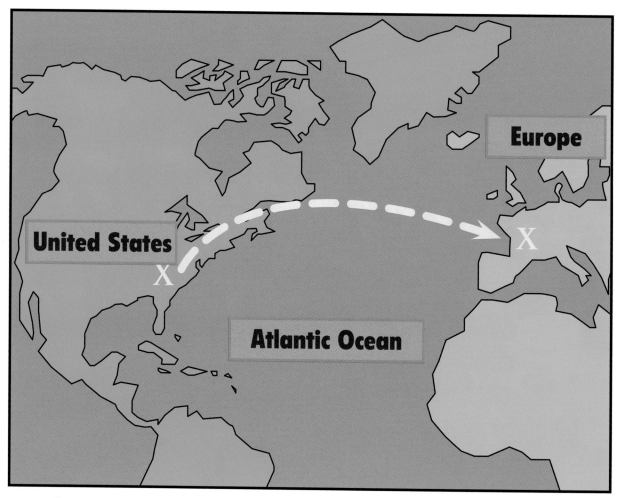

Amelia set one record in 1928. She became the first woman to cross the Atlantic Ocean in an airplane! A man named Wilmer Stultz flew the plane.

When Amelia and Wilmer got back to the United
States, the country gave them a big **parade**! People
were very proud of Amelia. This made her want
to fly again.

In 1932, Amelia set another important record. She flew
across the Atlantic Ocean all by herself! She was
the first woman to do this.

This trip was scary, but Amelia was very brave. When Amelia returned to the United States, the president gave her an **award**.

Amelia's trip made her famous. She showed the world that women could do things that men usually did.
A lot of women wanted to be like Amelia.

Amelia did many things that most people hadn't done before. She had a lot of courage. Courage means that you do things even if you're afraid.

Amelia's Last Trip

In 1937, Amelia wanted to set the hardest record she could think of. She wanted to be the first woman to fly around the world!

Amelia started her trip in July 1937. The trip was **dangerous**, but Amelia wasn't afraid. She said that it's important to do new things, even if they're scary.

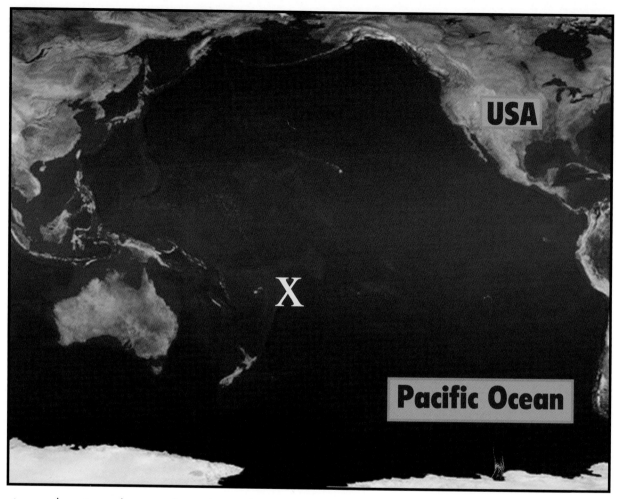

Amelia's plane broke down during her trip. Her plane **disappeared** when she was flying over the Pacific Ocean. Nobody was ever able to find her.

People have always wondered what happened to Amelia. Some people are still looking for her plane. Even though she was lost, we still remember her as a brave aviator.

Amelia's Records

1922	flew higher in the air than any other woman aviator
1928	first woman to cross the Atlantic Ocean in an airplane
1932	first woman to fly over the Atlantic Ocean by herself
1932	first woman to fly across the United States by herself
1935	first woman to fly over the Pacific Ocean by herself

Glossary

aviator (AY-vee-ay-tuhr) Someone who flies an airplane.

award (uh-WOHRD) Something given to honor something done well.

dangerous (DAYN-juh-ruhs) Full of danger.

disappear (dihs-uh-PEER) To go missing.

parade (puh-RAYD) A group of people marching together down a street.

popular (PAH-pyuh-luhr) Well-liked and well-known.

Index

around the world, 18

Atlantic Ocean, 12, 14,
    22

aviator, 5, 11, 21, 22

award, 15

courage, 17

disappeared, 20

flying classes, 9

Pacific Ocean, 20, 22

parade, 13

plane(s), 5, 6, 7, 8, 12,
    20, 21, 22

president, 15

record(s), 10, 11, 12, 14,
    18, 22

Stultz, Wilmer, 12, 13

United States, 12, 13, 15,
    22